The Miracle Of
GRACE

Also By The Author

9 Bible Principles for Judging Prophecy

101 Facts About Satanism In America

Being Happy In An Unhappy World

Communnication in Marriage

Should Christians Support Israel?

The Power To Heal

Bible Positions on Political Issues

12 Sunday Mornings with Pastor John Hagee

Vol. 1, Vol. 2, Vol. 3, & Vol. 4

Turn on The Light

ISBN # 156908 - 003 - 8

The Miracle Of
GRACE

John C. Hagee

First printing, July 1991.

Second printing, April 1995

THE MIRACLE OF GRACE© 1991 by John C. Hagee and Global Evangelism Television, Inc. All Rights reserved. Written by John Hagee; Edited by Connie Reece; Produced by Lucretia Hobb; Printed by Horticulture Printers, Dallas, Texas, USA. No part of this book may be used or reproduced in any manner whatsoever without the written permission, except in the case of brief quotations embodied in critical articles and reviews. For information write John Hagee Ministries, P.O. Box 1400, San Antonio, TX 78295.

Part 1
The Grace Killers

The Grace Killers

God's grace is both exciting and exasperating. It's exciting because grace opens the doors of freedom for a joyous, happy, victorious Christian life. It's exasperating because many evangelicals reject and ridicule grace as something that's just too good to be true. I want you to understand that God's grace is just as good as it sounds, even though many people do not understand what God's grace is all about.

At a church board meeting, one of the deacons objected to the pastor's recommendation that they buy a chandelier for the church. The deacon said, "I object to the chandelier because, first, nobody can even spell it to order it. Secondly, I object to it, because in this church no one can play it. And thirdly, I object to it because what we need in this church is more light."

The point is this: if you don't understand what grace is, you will not want to see it in action. I want to explain grace to you fully, so that the miracle of grace can become a reality in your life.

If you fear the freedom of grace, then you become a Grace Killer.

Every church in America has Grace Killers. They're the long-faced, unhappy 'God Squad' who go around making sure everybody keeps their set of rules. They're the people who want to manipulate you, and dominate you, and intimidate you with their religious rules. The Grace Killers want you to live up to their expectations. The Grace Killers are legalistic in their opinions. If you get into a grace-killing sewer of legalism, I guarantee you are going to live one hellish life. The grace of God is the only escape from that nightmare.

The grace of God will set you free. Free from what? Free from yourself. Some of you live in a penitentiary that you have constructed: you're a prisoner to the tyranny of other people's expectations, the tyranny of their opinions, and the tyranny of their demands. But God's grace will set you free...free to obey, free to love, free to forgive others, and free to forgive yourself. Some of you have never been able to forgive yourselves of the things that God has already forgiven you of long ago.

God's grace will set you free to allow people to be who they are, not what you think they ought to be. Do you allow people the gracious position of having an opinion that is different from yours? Good people can have differing opinions. When you and someone else have identical opinions, one of you is not necessary. If you force someone to see things exactly like you do on every occasion, you have cloned yourself, and God's grace cannot work in your life.

Some of you are are trapped on a performance treadmill. You're constantly suffering from the 'tyranny of oughts.' I ought to do this, I ought to do that. You're saved, you pray, you read the word of God, you witness—you are doing more and enjoying it less in the house of God. You are suffering on the edge of burn-out. You're bitter. You're physically and emotionally exhausted. You feel frustrated, defeated, and disillusioned. The only way you're ever going to experience a happy Christian life is through God's grace.

We're going to explore the exciting grace of God. Grace cannot be earned. Grace is greater than all of your sins. Grace keeps you...grace preserves you...grace delivers you...and grace will present you faultless before the Father on the day of judgment. Grace destroys fear. In the presence of grace, there is laughter and happiness.

God's grace has been freely given to everyone. But many of you say, "It's just too good to be true. I'll have to get my righteousness the old fashioned way—I'll just have to earn it." Give up! All of your righteousness is as filthy rags. The only way you're ever going to have joy and peace and happiness is to accept the free, unmerited favor of God today.

Ephesians 2:8 and 9 says,

For by grace are you saved through faith; and that not of yourselves: it is the gift of God: not of works, lest any man should boast.

This verse says you are saved by grace. **What is grace? Grace is the unmerited favor of God.** Favor is a synonym for grace.

Grace is free. You cannot do anything to earn the grace of God. If you can earn the grace of God, that's legalism—and legalism is the cornerstone for paganism. Every denomination in America has its own particular form of legalism, a set of rules that men make in order to obtain righteousness with God. Eating fish on Friday is legalism. You cannot find that in the word of God. No music in the church is legalism. That has nothing to do with the word of God. Wearing long hair and a long dress to obtain righteousness with God is Pentecostal legalism. It has nothing to do with the grace of God. Closed communion in a Baptist church is legalism. It has nothing to do with the grace of God.

You cannot earn the grace of God. You cannot do something to be holy. You have to accept what Jesus did on the cross, or live a life of pure misery. No one ever kept the law. Only those who accept the grace of God can live a happy and carefree life.

How does grace work? Grace works like this.
Imagine that you have one son. He's six years old and he's the apple of your eye. One day you come home and find that your son has been brutally murdered. Enraged, you call the police and then you help them find your son's killer. Now you have a choice. You can kill your son's murderer—that's *vengeance*. Or you can let the courts convict him and execute him—that's *justice*. It probably wouldn't happen that way in America, but that's how justice is supposed to work. Thirdly, you can plea for his pardon. You can forgive him completely, and after he's released from jail you can invite him into your home and adopt him as your only son—that's *grace*.

You say, "Preacher, that's impractical, unreasonable, and impossible." In the flesh it is, but through the miracle of God's grace nothing is impossible.

How were you saved by grace? God sent His only begotten son to the earth. He was murdered by the created, but God the Father adopted the killers of Christ to be His sons and daughters. That's you and me. I am a son of the living God. You are a member of the royal family of heaven. We are heirs and joint heirs with Jesus Christ. The royal blood of heaven flows in our veins. We have been created a little lower than the angels.

By the miracle of God's grace, all of my sin has been forgiven. As hymn writer William Cowper said, "There is a fountain filled with blood drawn from Immanuel's veins; and sinners, plunged beneath that flood, lose all their guilty stains." Accept the grace of the cross that forgives your sin, forgives your past. Look straight into the future and say, "Thank God, I'm saved by His amazing grace."

You see, you deserve to die, because you were born in sin. When Adam sinned in the garden, sin entered the world.

The Bible says, "by one man sin entered into the world." (Rom. 5:12) The Bible also says that the wages of sin is death. (Rom. 6:23)

When you opened your eyes on this earth, you were already a sinner. Therefore, a death sentence for you is justice. Justice would have been served had God allowed us to die in our sin. But it was an act of God's grace to send Jesus to die on the cross to save us. That means I am now free by the grace of God to forgive the guilt of the past. I am free from the fear of the future. I am free from the feeble expectations of other people. I am free from the demands and opinions of other people. I am free to live. I am free to love. I am free to laugh. I am free to be happy. I am set free by the grace of God, and whom the Son sets free is free indeed. (John 8:36)

"For by grace are you saved." **Those are beautiful words: saved by grace.** Saved from what? I am saved from the pain and the penalty of sin. I am saved from Satan, the roaring lion seeking whom he may devour. The Lion of Judah has conquered the roaring lion from hell and gives me the free grace of the cross that makes me absolutely bulletproof against the powers and principalities of hell.

I'm saved from the flames of an eternal hell. I'm saved from everlasting death. When I stand up and say, "I'm a sinner saved by grace," it is the most exciting pronouncement a mortal can make. I could not joyfully say I'm the President of the United States. I could not joyfully say I'd been appointed to the United Nations. But I can say with great joy that I am a sinner saved by grace. I'm a child of God, a member of the royal family of heaven, an heir and a joint heir with Jesus Christ. I own it all—hallelujah!

Because of the miracle of God's grace at Calvary, Jesus took my death sentence. I deserved to die, but He took my death and He gave me everlasting life. I didn't earn it. I didn't deserve it. But God's free grace gave it to me.

He took my sicknesses and my disease and He gave me health and healing. He took my judgment and gave me God's goodness and mercy. He took my crown of thorns and He gave me the crown of glory. He took my rejection and He gave me God's approval.

And when His blood-soaked head fell upon His chest and He said, "It is finished," every demon in hell ran to the caverns of the deep and Satan trembled in terror. In that instant the God of all grace took a parchment of human flesh, the flesh of His Son, and wrote on it with the ink of His blood, SAVED BY GRACE. He rolled up the parchment and placed it in my hand. And now when Satan, the roaring lion, comes to my house and says, "you're not worthy of the grace of God... you're not worthy of the grace of God...you're not worthy of the grace of God," I open this precious text and I hear it say, "you are saved by the grace of God." I look hell's legions in the eye and say, "I am redeemed. I am justified as if I never sinned. My sins are all forgiven, buried in the deepest sea never to be remembered against me anymore. I am saved by the grace of the almighty, eternal, sovereign God. Get out of my face, devil, I am a child of the King."

You are a trophy of God's grace. Get hold of that thought. You are a magnificent specimen of His saving grace, of His keeping grace, of His "amazing grace, how sweet the sound."

Why was grace necessary? One word—sin. In the Genesis, a perfect God created a perfect world with perfect humans. Adam and Eve had a perfect marriage. Adam didn't have to hear about all the men she could have married. Eve didn't have to hear about what a great cook his mother was. When Eve asked Adam, "Do you love me?" Adam said, "who else Eve, who else?"

It was a perfect marriage. But Satan, the father of lies, the master of deception, could not stand the joy and the peace and the unity of the human family that God had created, a family that worshiped only God. So he slithered into the Garden of Eden and he attacked the minds of Adam and Eve by saying, "Hath God said?...Does the word of God really mean this?"

When Satan comes to destroy you, the first thing he will attack is your mind. Everything that's going wrong in America today stems from an attack on our minds. Drug abuse is an attack on the mind. Alcoholism destroys the mind. Pornography attacks the mind. Current medical studies verify that when you see a pornographic picture, enzymes are released in the brain that burn the pornographic image into your cells. Pornography attacks the mind and it stays there. Witchcraft attacks the mind. Satanism, humanism, and New Age thought attack the mind. ESP and Eastern philosophy attack the mind.

How do you combat this attack on your mind? The Bible

says, "Let this mind be in you, which was also in Christ Jesus." (Philippians 2:5) The Bible also says that we must renew our minds. (Romans 12:2)

Sin begins in your mind before it becomes a fact. Sin has three stages. It begins as a fascination. And then it takes a form. And then it becomes a fact.

Murder does not begin when you shoot the gun. Murder begins when you allow your brain to swim in the sewer of hatred. Adultery does not begin with a date in Motel Six. It begins when you allow your mind to swim in the sewer of lust. Divorce does not begin when you hire a lawyer. It begins when you fantasize what life would be like without your spouse. Suicide does not begin when you buy the pills for an overdose. It begins when you think, "I wish I were not alive." Death is a spirit, and you can invite the spirit of death to take you over. When you say with your mouth, "I wish I were not alive," you summon the spirit of death.

The Bible says, "to him that *knoweth*"— see the mind in that. "To him that knoweth to do good, and doeth it not, to him it is sin." (James 4:17) What do you think about? That's what you are. And that's what you're going to do. For that reason, on the day of judgment, you will give an account to God for every thought you think. The Bible says "casting down imaginations"—that's your thought life, "and every high thing that exalteth itself against the knowledge of God...bringing into captivity every thought to the obedience of Christ." (II Corinthians 10:5)

Let's go back to the fall of man in the garden. **If I talked all day, I could not explain the significance of what was lost when Adam and Eve disobeyed God.** When Adam and Eve disobeyed God, their sin, and all that it implied, was passed to you and me. That's why you hear God in the garden saying, "Adam, where art thou? Where art thou?" When I was a young preacher I imagined God saying, "Adam you dumbbell. I created a perfect paradise for you and you botched it...now get out of here!" But as I have studied the word of God for thirty-three years, I hear God saying "Adam, Adam, Adam. Do you know what you've done? Do you understand the power of sin that you've unleashed on all of humanity from this day forward? Because of what you have done, my Son will now have to die so that men can have a chance to recapture what you have just destroyed. Adam, I created you to have everlasting life. Now death has been released. I created you with perfect health. Now sickness has been released. We had perfect companionship, Adam. Now man is forever separated from me. We had a perfect world, Adam. Now there are thorns on every rose and Johnson grass is growing everywhere." When you cut the grass the next time, say a special prayer for Adam.

The earth is a spiritual creation. Romans 8:22 says the whole world is groaning in the pains of child birth. Every earthquake, every storm, every flood, every tornado, every volcanic eruption is a convulsion of nature, which is out of balance and out of harmony with God's perfect will because of sin. Insurance companies call hurricanes and tornadoes 'acts of God.' That's exactly backwards. Hurricanes and tornadoes are the end result of sin manifested in nature.

We lost physical perfection when Adam sinned. Adam was a Superman and Eve was a ravishing number 10, as God created them in the Garden of Eden. Now people who are very imperfect physically are down at the health spa every day trying to gain back what Adam threw away in the garden. Generations of disease and deformities and deterioration and death have provided physical imperfection. Every pair of eye glasses is a testimonial to physical imperfection. Every set of false teeth is a testimonial to physical imperfection. Look at yourself in the mirror and say, "Is this physical perfection?" I think not. Adam lost it for us.

We lost mental perfection in the garden. Adam was a mental genius who named every creature on earth. He was the first and only General Manager of the Universe. What a memory he had to name every living creature, tens of thousands of them. But sin destroyed our mental perfection. Now we tie a string around our finger and forget why we tied the string there.

We lost emotional perfection. There was no worry or fear or dread or anger or bitterness or retaliation or resentment in the garden. Sin brought that. Sin is the basis for every argument in your marriage. Sin is the basis for your anxiety over things you cannot control.

We lost relational perfection. Adam and Eve had a beautiful openness in the garden. They were not fearful of each other. The first thing they did when they sinned was to hide from each other, and we've been hiding ever since. We hide behind emotional masks, afraid to be ourselves. We hide behind religious masks, fearful of the Grace Killers that stalk every church making sure everyone else keeps their religious rules. Family unity becomes a greater and greater struggle because of the fact that we have lost that relational perfection. Grace alone can bring it back.

There is lurking within the soul of man the deep desire to regain the perfection we lost in the Garden of Eden. And that perfection we lost in the Garden of Eden *can* be regained. It can be regained the moment you give up trying to do it in your own flesh and accept the miracle of God's grace.

By grace, God can give you perfect peace. He can give you perfect joy. He can give you perfect relationships. He can give you freedom that the world knows nothing about. The moment that you say,"Father, in Jesus' name, I am not going to be a people pleaser. I am not going to be mastered or manipulated by the opinions and the dictates and the expectations of the Grace Killers. I am going to please You. I will walk according to Your word and Your grace"—in that moment you step back into the Garden of Eden, and Satan and all of his little helpers can't molest you. You can have the peace that surpasses all understanding. You can live a victorious, happy Christian life through the miracle of God's grace.

There are three major hindrances to God's grace. The first is the performance trap. You think God loves you because of what you do. That's wrong. Nothing you will ever do will make you precious in the eyes of God other than Jesus Christ and His sacrifice.

Some of you are trying to gain the approval of others by what you do. Believe me, Jesus couldn't please people, Paul couldn't please people, and you can't please people. So give it up and tell the Grace Killers to take a hike.

Christians caught in the performance trap say, "I'm getting my righteousness the old fashioned way. I'm going to earn it. I'm an Avis Christian—I try harder."

Christians caught in the performance trap are sincere. They're highly motivated. They're extremely hard working people. But they're trapped on the treadmill of performance. They live in bondage, and they think the only way out is to try a little harder...if they're working 8 hours, to work 10 hours, 12 hours, 14 hours, 16 hours...work a little harder, and a little harder, and a little harder, and they go faster and faster until they emotionally collapse.

God doesn't love you more because you do more. God loves you because of what Jesus did at the cross.

Works will not save you. Your works are evidence of how much you love God. But what Jesus did at the cross is evidence of how much God loves you. You're saved because of what Jesus did at the cross. If you do nothing, God still loves you. He doesn't want you to do nothing...if you do nothing you won't have His approval...but He still loves you.

Works will not save you. Some of you are going to three Bible studies a week and you only drink carrot juice, bless God, because you're going to get to heaven (if you don't jog right by the gates of glory) because, bless God, you're going to earn salvation in Jesus' name. Give it up! **Nothing you can do will earn your salvation. You see, that's why grace is so easy.** Just accept what Jesus did.

Now there's a difference between believing and confessing. Someone who is lost can only come to grace by believing. "Believe on the Lord Jesus Christ, and thou shalt be saved." (Acts 16:31) Confessing is what someone who is saved does. When you are already saved and you have sinned, then you confess your sin, and God forgives you and renews that relationship. "If we confess our sins, he is faithful and just to forgive us our sins, and to cleanse us from all unrighteousness." (I John 1:9)

People mistakenly say, "I'm growing in grace." Let me show how that's wrong. If I dive in the Gulf of Mexico, the Gulf of Mexico is not threatened. God's grace is like an ocean. It's bottomless, it's shoreless, it's infinite. Grace can grow in me, but the idea that I'm growing in grace is not exactly right. I become more gracious as I allow God to get the carnal man out of me, but I am not growing in grace, because grace is infinite.

Here are nine signs that you are caught in the performance trap. One, you're never at peace. Secondly, you're afraid of making mistakes. Thirdly, you always feel anxiety. Four and five, you feel guilt and condemnation. Six, you're dominated by anger. Anger is always in your speech and you have smoldering resentments that never are resolved. Seven, you have outbursts of rage. Eight, you have excessive mood swings that go from one side of the spectrum completely to the other. Nine, you are suffering from depression. If you are a performance-trap Christian, you need to stop and say, "I am going to be free in the name of Jesus, and by the miracle of grace, I'm getting off this merry-go-round and live with the joy of God."

The second hindrance to grace is individualism. These are the John Wayne or Annie Oakley Christians who say, "I can handle this all by myself. I'm a tongues-talking, Bible-carrying, King James-version-quoting Christian and I can handle this crisis all by myself." Let me tell you what's going to happen to you. You will find a problem some day that you can't solve. And you're going to fail miserably. Your nose is going to be ignominiously introduced to the dirt as you fall flat on your face. And then you'll have a choice. You either have to admit, "I failed and I'm asking for the grace of God to help me get up again." Or you're going to get up, dust yourself off, and go back to church and pretend nothing ever happened. If you do that, you'll bury that problem deeply in your emotions and in your thoughts. That problem will fester like a sore, and it will stay there until it rots your soul.

Let me tell you something, my fair-feathered, Bible-carrying, self-righteous, little Grace Killer. Sooner or later you're going to run into a problem that will eat your lunch. And when you do, you'd better run to the cross and plead for the grace of God. And God will give it to you—you will get up off your knees whiter than snow and stronger than you've ever been. If you do anything other than that, your life will be a living hell. Don't strut yourself like a peacock and say, "I can handle it." You can't handle it. That's why Jesus Christ had to go to the cross.

The third hindrance to grace is legalism, the keeping of manmade rules to obtain righteousness with God. Legalism is Satan's theology in the church, wherein Satan controls the church by manmade rules and not the rules of God.

God hates legalism. Why? Because if you can keep rules to obtain righteousness with God, Calvary is a farce and Jesus died in vain. The legalists in Jesus' day were the Pharisees, and the Pharisees have become the legalistic Grace Killers of the 20th century...hard, cold, bitter, loveless, mean-spirited, peacock-proud, Bible-thumping 'God Squads' that make sure everybody keeps their religious rules. These modern Pharisees kill joy. They kill freedom. And they kill love. They kill with their words, they kill with their self-righteous looks, they kill with their vindictive attitudes. Let me ask you this, Mr. Grace Killer, who are you to tell humanity how to live? Who made you god of the universe? The Bible says, "Judge not, that you be not judged." (Matthew 7:1)

John 1:17 says, "For the law was given by Moses, but grace and truth came by Jesus Christ." Grace made its appearance in Bethlehem's manger. Grace, in the form of Jesus, was dropped into a world filled with the legalism of the Pharisees. Did the Pharisees love Jesus? No, they hated him. Grace Killers who can't control you will hate you.

Jesus said the Pharisees had made the traditions of men of more importance than the word of God. (Mark 7:6-9) That's happening right now, in the 20th century, right here in America. Denominations have church rules that they keep above all else, even above the word of God. If most denominations quit doing what's out of balance with the word of God, you wouldn't recognize what they do next Sunday in your church.

God hates legalism, because legalism destroys grace. Does the grace of Jesus live in you? Or have you become a Grace Killer?

To show grace is to extend kindness to one who does not deserve it. That's what grace is. To show favor or kindness to someone who does not deserve it and who could never earn it. Consider Jesus and the woman who was caught in the act of adultery. (John 8:1-11) The Pharisees brought the woman to Jesus. The Grace Killers said, "Stone her." Jesus, who had grace and truth, said "Let her live."

Listen to me—if all you're doing is keeping the law, you'll always be within your rights to hurt somebody else. And if all that you're out to do is preserve your rights, you're going to live in a hell on earth. That's why America is such a painful nation to live in, because every minority and every political interest group is screaming about "my rights." But Jesus said the way to regain paradise is to grant favor to people who don't deserve it and could never earn it. If you want your marriage to be heaven on earth, allow your spouse to have a difference of opinion. Don't eat their lunch because they don't see what you see. In that freedom there is a new basis for love and relationship.

Jesus extended favor to those that didn't deserve it. When Lazarus died, Mary and Martha met Jesus on the road. They said, "If you'd been here, our brother wouldn't have died." Do you hear the accusation in that? "Preacher, if you'd been doing what you were supposed to do, this wouldn't have

happened." How many times have I heard that?
Jesus, full of grace, did not even reply to Mary's and Martha's accusations. What about you? When someone hangs their teeth in you, do you turn around and verbally backhand them? Or do you extend grace?

Jesus also told a story about the prodigal son. (Luke 15:11-32) A Jewish boy who dishonored his father—that was enough to be disinherited. A Jewish boy who wasted all his family's wealth—that was a worse sin. But a Jewish boy who became the keeper of pigs—that was unthinkable! When the prodigal son came home, his father gave him the best robe, saying, "All of your past is forgiven." He gave him shoes, saying, "You're not a slave, but a son." (It was against the law for a slave to wear shoes.) And he gave him the signet ring, giving the son authority over everything the father owned.

I want you to understand that this God who is perfect has given to every one of us free grace that is greater than all our sin. It's greater than any nightmare you're going through. You may not feel you deserve grace. That feeling in and of itself comes straight out of hell, because Jesus said, "whosoever will, let him take the water of life freely." (Rev. 22:17)

If you are trapped in a prison that you have created, or a prison you've allowed other Grace Killers to create, you need to walk out of that prison and receive the free grace, the miracle-working grace, the saving and keeping grace, of a gracious God.

If your attitudes are negative, judgmental and loveless, and your emotions are filled with anger, resentment, bitterness, and fear, let the Lord supernaturally put His arms around you and let you feel His amazing grace.

If you're a Christian caught in the performance trap, working to please God and receive the approval of other people, ask God today, in Jesus' name, to help you get off this performance treadmill.

If you're suffering from individualism and you have deep, hidden problems you're fearful of confessing, ask the Lord today, in Jesus' name, to give you the strength to cry out for His free grace.

If you're saved but you're not gracious—you do not extend favor to people unless they deserve it—ask the Lord today to make you a gracious Christian.

If you're a good, moral person, but you've never received Jesus, that means you're lost. Lost—there is no hope! Receive Jesus into your heart today.

Pray this prayer with me:
Lord Jesus Christ, I ask you to forgive all of my sin and cleanse me from all unrighteousness. Lord Jesus Christ, today, in Jesus' name, I receive the miracle of your grace. All of my sins are forgiven. I am free from the opinions, the dictates and the demands of other people. I'm free to love you and to serve you. I'm free to forgive myself. I'm free from the performance trap. I'm free from legalism. I'm liberated from individualism. I am saved and justified by the grace of God. In Jesus' name, I am free to experience the miracle of God's grace in my life."

Part 2
Grace That Yields

Grace That Yields

Grace is the unmerited favor of God. Grace is favor and favor is grace.

The miracle of God's grace will set you free. Any area of your life that is not free is in darkness. And where there is darkness, Satan rules. No one is as free as Jesus died to make them. The Bible says, "Whom the Son sets free is free indeed." (John 8:36)

Grace will set you free from yourself. It will set you free from other people. It will set you free to live in the liberty of God.

God's grace is greater than all of your sins. Grace saves you, grace delivers you and grace will sustain you.

Romans 6:13-16 says:

Neither yield...your members as instruments of unrighteousness under sin: but yield yourselves unto God, as those that are alive from the dead, and your members as instruments of righteousness under God. For sin shall not have dominion over you: for you are not under the law, but under grace. What then? shall we sin, because we are not under the law, but under grace? God forbid. Know you not, that to whom you yield yourselves servants to obey, his servants you are to whom you obey; whether of sin unto death, or of obedience unto righteousness?

Isn't grace dangerous? **That's the supreme question of this text.**

Most evangelicals fear grace. The moment a preacher gets up in the pulpit and says, "God's grace is greater than all of your sins," someone will say, "Well, if you're telling people that God's grace is greater than their sin, won't they just continue to sin?"

Tragically, there are some people who say, "What's a little adultery? I'm living under the grace of God. What's a little lying?" But God's grace is not a license to sin. Not at all.

Paul said in Romans 6:1, "Are we to continue in sin that grace may abound?" And he answers, "God forbid." Are we to go on sinning in order to prove how wonderful God's grace is? No. The fact is, where there is a choice of liberty, which is grace, or bondage, which is legalism, there will always be people who choose to be extremists. There are people who are looking for a way to justify their sins and there are people who are looking for a way to justify their extreme religiosity.

God's grace makes me free from manmade rules, but I am not free from the word of God. God expects me to repent and change. Jesus told the woman caught in adultery, "Go and sin no more." If there is no change, there is no repentance.

There is a difference between "greasy" grace and God's grace. "Greasy" grace justifies the sin; God's grace justifies the sinner. Jesus Christ was tough on sin but compassionate towards the sinner. The church has turned that around. We've become hard on people and easy on the issue. We need to see it like Jesus saw it: tough on the sin and easy on the sinner.

By the miracle of grace I am justified before God. Now, what is justification? Almost any Christian can tell you, justification means just as if I'd never sinned. That's right, but that definition is too shallow to explain what justification is all about.

Justification is a forensic term. It is a term always used in a legal setting. When a prisoner is brought before the courts, there's only one way he can be justified: he must be found innocent. If he's found guilty, he can never be justified.

If I go out and shoot someone and I'm found guilty, the President can pardon me. I'm still a killer, I just have a pardon. But I can never be justified, because I've been found guilty. Let that sink in. If you're ever found guilty, you can't be justified in the courts.

Now, you and I have been found guilty of sin. The Bible says, "All have sinned and come short of the glory of God." (Romans 3:23) Yet the Bible also says I am justified by faith. (Romans 3:28) How can I be justified if I've already been found guilty?

There are complicated answers for this, but I want to give you an answer that even a child can understand. In the theater of your mind go with me to a courtroom. A prisoner has been tried. He's been found guilty. He's been condemned to death. He cannot be justified, because he is guilty.

But suppose a second man comes into the room and says,

"I will take that man's guilt upon myself. I will serve his sentence." He becomes a substitute for the guilty man. In a human court, this man can serve my sentence, but he can't take away the shame of my crime. He can take my punishment, but he can't justify me. He can take my punishment, but it will not remove my guilt.

Now, what flesh and blood cannot do is exactly what Jesus Christ has done. He took my place on the cross. He didn't just take my punishment, He took my guilt when He died. When Jesus went to the cross, I went to the cross. When He died, I died. When He came out of the grave, I came out of the grave.

Because I've accepted Jesus as my substitute, I'm not just somebody walking around with a piece of paper saying I'm pardoned. I am a new human being. A new creature. The old guy that committed all of those sins, he's in the grave, he's dead. So in the courts of heaven, it's as if I never sinned. Because the guy who did the sin is in the grave.

That's why, when you get baptized and you break that water, all of your sin, all of your trangressions, all of your unthinkable, unholy past is buried in that watery grave. You come out of the water a brand new creature. The world has never seen you before. Heaven has never seen you before. When God looks down from the balcony of heaven He says, "There is a brand new creature in Christ Jesus…whiter than the driven snow…justified by his faith in Jesus Christ. There's not one sin or transgression on his record. He is justified by the grace of My Son."

The evidence that God's grace rules in your heart is the ability to yield to the will of God and to the needs of other people.

While we are to yield first to God, and then to others, there are some things to which we must never yield ourselves. First of all, we are not to yield to the devil. The Bible says, "resist the devil and he will flee from you." (James 4:7) Paul said in Ephesians 6, "We wrestle not against flesh and blood." "We wrestle not" defines what some Christians do— they just don't wrestle. They're not into resisting the devil. They're not into resisting the wicked.

But hear this. The church of Jesus Christ is at war with the powers and principalities in the heavens. There is no compromise with the world, the flesh, or the devil. You will either live according to the dictates of God, or according to the dictates of a humanistic society. I, for one, have chosen to be loyal to my Commander in Chief, the Lord Jesus Christ who has saved me by His grace. I have determined to be a soldier in the army of the Lord and to be victorious in the name of my Blessed Redeemer. I have chosen to be a victor and not a victim. I am going to stand before the throne of grace by His sovereign love and announce, "Jesus Christ is Lord to the glory of God the Father." Satan's mad and I'm glad the victory is ours, in Jesus' name.

The Bible also says we're not to yield ourselves to sin. We're also not to yield ourselves to self pity. Self pity is the road to addiction and suicide. Every person that has gotten hooked on alcohol and drugs got there by self pity. "Look what my mother did to me. Look what my father did to me. Look what my pastor, my church or what God did to me." Let me tell you something. You are in sin because you decided to be sinful. You are doing what you are doing because you made the decision and your choices have consequences. You need to wake up to that fact and get off your pity pot and live your life in the grace of God.

Don't yield yourself to resentment. Resentment is cyanide to your soul. Don't yield yourself to jealousy. Jealousy is more cruel than the grave. Don't yield yourself to bitterness, because bitterness is the father of divorce. It is the father of division and depression. Many of you live in constant depression. You could not live without Valium or some other medical prescription, because you constantly rehearse the bitter scenes of your life. A bitter divorce, a bitter memory, a hurtful happening. You go over it, and over it, and over it, and over it in your mind. It will choke your soul like a rotten cancer chokes out healthy tissues. God's word calls it "a root of bitterness" and it will destroy God's grace in your life. (Hebrews 12:15)

You have surrendered your mind to Satan himself when all you choose to do is to remember the unhappy past. Paul said, "forgetting those things which are behind, and reaching forth unto those things which are before, I press toward the mark for the prize of the high calling of God in Christ Jesus." (Phil. 3:13-14) There is "joy unspeakable and full of glory" in Christ the Lord. I am more than a conqueror through Christ.

So we do not yield ourselves to sin or to the devil. But we are to yield ourselves to God's will and the needs of others.

The evidence of grace operating in your life is the ability to yield yourself to the will of God and to the needs of others.

Grace is giving mercy to the unmerciful. Grace is giving kindness to the unkind. Grace is giving goodness to the totally bad. Grace is giving salvation to those who don't deserve to be saved.

Paul writes in Romans 15:1, "We then that are strong ought to bear the infirmities of the weak and not to please ourselves." If there is any weakness in the mind, in the body or in the emotions of another person, you are to bear that weakness. That's how you determine how spiritually strong you are, by your ability to bear the weaknesses of other people.

Are there some people that just really bug you? Maybe you're married to one of them. Some people just have a talent for irritating you beyond words.

A woman on a bus kept walking up the aisle saying "Where's my street, where do I get off?" The bus driver told her over and over where she would get off. After she came up the aisle the umpteenth time and said, "How am I going to know where to get off this bus?" the driver hollered at her, "Lady, you'll know where to get off this bus by the big smile on my face!"

Some people have the ability to irritate you. But God says, in Romans 15, if they are feeble in any sense, whether mind, body, or spirit, your grace factor is measured by your ability to put up with that weakness.

America's attitude seems to be "let the powerful rule and let the weak be thrown out with the garbage." Hitler had that attitude. The communists have that attitude. And America has adopted that attitude.

That's the attitude that makes abortion possible. A baby in the womb is too weak to fight off the forceps that rip its body to a bloody pulp. It's too weak to fight off the saline solution that drowns it. It can't vote us out of office, and it can't fight back. So who cares?

Let me tell you something—God cares. And just for the record, every doctor and every nurse who is participating in the abortion mills of America will stand before God Almighty convicted of murder in the first degree. They will walk the corridors of hell forever wishing they had never been a part of it.

I'm talking about the attitude "let the powerful rule and

let the weak be devoured." Rapists and child molesters have that mentality. Women in America are afraid to walk on city streets at night because there is so much danger of attack. Women and children are too weak to fight off the sexual advances of the rapist and the child molester.

I've got news for the rapists and child molesters. The American judicial system may be too weak to bring you to justice, but God's judicial system is not. You may be getting by with it right now, but you won't get by with it forever. God says He will shout from the housetops what you've tried to do in secret. (Luke 12:3) God has your "most wanted" mugshot on his bulletin board in heaven and He's going to take it up with you on the day of judgment.

Every woman needs to hear this. If you have a husband who is sexually abusing your daughter or son, turn him over to the cops and lock him up. Doing anything else falls short of the grace of God.

I'm talking about the attitude "let the powerful rule and let the weak be devoured." We have a whole generation of senior citizens in rest homes, sitting day in and day out in a sedated stupor, waiting for death to come. I visited a white-haired mother in a rest home the other day. She said, "Pastor, would you ask my son to come visit me?" Thinking he surely must be in Europe or Outer Mongolia, I said, "Where does your son live?" She said, "He lives six blocks from here." I said, "When did he come to see you last?" She said it had been over a year.

That is sin. That's wrong. The Bible says, "Honor your father and mother...that it may be well with you." (Ephesians 6:2-3) If you don't honor them, it will not be well with you. God will see to that. I don't see how one man and one woman can raise six children and those six children grow up and cannot take care of that one man and that one woman. That kind of caring must return to this nation before this nation can be great again.

God never writes anybody off. David said, "Lord, if you count our iniquities who can stand?" (Psalm 130:3) The first century Christians did not write off the prostitutes, the tax collectors, the lepers. The first man who walked into the gates of heaven was a criminal saved at Calvary by the blood of Jesus Christ. Jesus didn't look over at him and say, "you're not the right kind of folks." He entered the gates of heaven covered by the blood of Christ.

Romans 15:1 not only says we are to bear the infirmities of the weak, we are "not to please ourselves." The church in America has become obsessed with attracting the right kind of people. What nonsense. The church of Jesus Christ is not a country club for religious fat cats. It is a hospital for hurting, broken people. It is a lighthouse for people who are stumbling in the darkness of sin, a beacon for those looking for a new direction. This is a place of healing, of love and compassion, a haven of rest for every man—of any color, any creed, any addiction—who is seeking an answer in God. We're in this church to save souls, not skins. If you're a racist and the color of somebody's skin irritates you, BUG OFF. We're not looking for your kind.

If you're in this church today and your life is broken, it's crushed...you feel like you've been chewed up and spit out with the garbage, then you're "the right kind of people." You're just who we're looking for. We want to tell you that God will heal you...He will save you...He will restore you...He will put your life back together again...He will cause you to sing again...He will give you "joy unspeakable and full of glory." He can make you a new creature in Christ Jesus. He will justify you and present you before the Father and His angels, saying, "Brand new, from head to toe...meet a child in the Kingdom of God!"

Worshipping the god of self has destroyed our nation. Self is a god, and if you worship the god of self, you are in deep idolatry. The attitude in America is "get all you can, and can all you get." We're losing our dimension of greatness because we have become a graceless, greedy, hedonistic society, living only to please ourselves, devoid of truth and responsibility.

A woman in New York City was brutally stabbed to death in her apartment. Her murderer came in and started stabbing her and she screamed for help. The murderer ran out, thinking the neighbors would come to help her. When no one came, he went back and finished killing her. He stabbed her ninety-six times. The police report showed that 26 people had heard the woman screaming for help. But not one of them came to her assistance.

What's happened to our ability to care one for the other? How did we lose our sensitivity for the needs of others?

Worshipping the god of self has corrupted, if not destroyed, the marriage fabric in this country. I listened to a song the other day and the words irritated me so much that I wrote them down. *Gentle On My Mind* —a song that some of you probably know very well. You don't know John 3:16, but you know *Gentle On My Mind*. The words go something like this—"It's not the ink stains dried on the marriage contract that keeps my bed roll behind the couch. It's knowing that I can get up and leave any time I want to. That's what keeps you gentle on my mind." The message is this: "You don't have any hooks in my hide just because we're married. If I get the urge to go, I go. Me and my rights, I am off. I expect you, lady, to stand in the doorway and wave goodbye to me...not knowing who the father of the new baby is...not knowing who will pay the rent or buy the food, or take care of the medical bills or who will help you when a crisis comes. I'm just so glad that you are 'gentle on my mind.'"

That is pure hogwash. I don't know a woman dumb enough in the world to buy that. And if you are, don't come up and introduce yourself to me. Let me live in my illusion!

Luke 9:23 says the cost of discipleship is the crucifixion itself. "If any man will come after me, let him deny himself, and take up his cross daily, and follow me."

Step one in exhibiting the grace and truth of the Lord is self-denial. Is that the mood of America? No. Is that the mood of the church? No.

Just imagine, if you will, that I announce we are going to have a self-denial crusade. How many people do you think would come? Nobody. If I announced a miracle campaign or a success and riches campaign, you'd have to get there early to get a seat. But if I said we were going to have a self-denial campaign—goodness, you'd have to get a bloodhound to find some people.

Step number two: "Take up your cross." Where is your cross? It's where your will and the will of God intersect. When your opinion goes this way and God's opinion goes that way, that's where your cross is. If you follow your opinion instead of God's opinion, you're into the idolatry of self.

Thirdly, "follow me." Jesus knows where to go. He knows the way through the wilderness. All you have to do is follow.

A man said to me the other day, "My life is going nowhere." I asked him, "Have you ever tried following a parked car?" He looked at me blankly. I said, "You're following your own self. You're going in circles. You're going in circles faster and faster, and you're calling that progress."

Do not confuse motion with progress. If you're not following Jesus, you're following the wrong force. If you're following your instincts, they will lead you astray.

Isaiah said you will hear a word behind you, saying, "This is the way, walk ye in it." (Isa. 30:21) Why do you hear a voice behind you? It means that you, as a sheep, have gone around the shepherd. You are doing your own thing and you are headed into a deep ditch. You are going to be lunch bait for a wolf unless you get back behind the shepherd.

Jesus said "no man takes [my life] from me, but I lay it down of myself." (John 10:18) You have to lay your life down for yourself. I Corinthians 1:25 says "the foolishness of God is wiser than men; and the weakness of God is stronger than men." That's a paradox. By the foolishness of the cross, God demonstrated grace and power. Why grace *and* power? If you only give a man power, he'll start abusing other people. You've heard the saying "power corrupts; absolute power corrupts absolutely." It's true. Grace stems the abuse of power. Jesus had all power in heaven and in earth. And when He was on the cross He had such grace, such composure, that when they spit on Him and beat Him and then killed Him, He used His last breath to pray for them. That's grace.

Does that describe your attitude? Or do you have the attitude "I'm going to have it my way. I don't care who I have to run over, what I have to do, and whose lunch I have to eat. I am the Righteous Rambo of my house, and it's going to happen my way, or hit the highway."

How is your attitude? Paul, who was beaten and stoned, shipwrecked and left for dead, graciously referred to his troubles as "these light afflictions." You say, "Pastor, Jesus was God. He said those kind of things." Yet Paul was very much a man like you and me, and he endured all of those things with grace and truth.

Romans 8:8 says, "They that are in the flesh cannot please God." But verse 9 says, "you are not in the flesh, but in the Spirit, if so be the Spirit of God dwell in you. Now if any man have not the spirit of Christ, he is none of his." What is the mark of the spirit of Christ? The Bible says that Jesus was full of grace and truth. **The distinctive mark that Jesus rules your life is that you have grace and**

truth—not tongues, not signs and wonders, not miracles, but grace. Grace that when somebody spits on you, you can retain your composure...that when the Roman soldier slaps you and mocks you, you can retain your composure.

Does that describe you? Or are you going through life demanding that everyone give you what you want?

Demanding, self-centered Christians have stormed the gates of heaven with their faith formulas, saying "I believe. I believe." Yes, but with what attitude do you believe? Let me tell you something, the Bible says that the demons believe, and they tremble. If all you do as a so-called Christian is believe and tremble, you do nothing more than demons do.

Your spiritual greatness is not marked by what you can believe. It is not marked by your emotions. It is marked by what you can do. James 1:22 says "Be ye doers of the word, and not hearers only." Jesus said, "You are my friends, if you do whatsoever I command you." (John 15:14)

Very soon the church is going to come to spiritual maturity. People are going to quit looking for hype in the pulpit, and start looking for integrity. They're going to stop looking for signs and wonders and start looking for the grace and truth of Jesus Christ in their pastor and in his ministry. That's the distinguishing mark between those who are following Christ and those who are not. Jesus was full of grace and truth.

In First Kings, chapter 3, God appeared to Solomon and said, "Ask me for what you will." Solomon didn't ask God for wealth; he asked Him for wisdom. Some time later, two prostitutes came to Solomon's court with one baby. Both prostitutes had had babies, but one of them in the night had rolled over on her baby and suffocated it. So she stole the other woman's baby, then went before Solomon and claimed the baby still alive as her own.

Here you've got two women claiming one baby. So Solomon took the baby by the heels, called for a sword, and was ready to hack it in half. The real mother said, "Give my baby to that woman." The point is this: if you really love the baby, you'd rather give the baby up than see the baby die. You will yield your will for the betterment of that which you love. What did the other prostitute say? "Cut it in half. I don't care about that baby, I want my half."

Now apply that to the family. There are marriages where

some of you are saying, "I'm going to have my way, and if I can't have my way, then cut it in half. Get a lawyer and rip it in half. I don't care what happens, it's got to be that way."

There are some of you that are involved in church matters, and you're saying, "If the church can't see my point of view, rip it in half. I'm going to have my way."

Right now America is being devastated by interest groups who are not interested in the country. They're interested in their own selfish, greedy, grabby, hedonistic instincts. As a nation we are disintegrating, because we have lost the sense of grace and truth that Jesus Christ taught us.

The yielding spirit brings your inheritance. The commanding spirit destroys what God has for you.

God called Abraham to be the father of many nations, and the father of all who believe. A more astute, spiritual person cannot be found in scripture. Abraham took his nephew Lot with him into the land of Canaan—it was a mistake. When they got out on the fields, Lot's herdsmen and Abraham's herdsmen began to argue with each other. Because they were bickering, Abraham went to his nephew and said, "You choose which way you want to go, and I will go in the opposite direction."

Now they lived in an Eastern culture. Abraham is the oldest. He is the senior member. By their social standards, Abraham had every right to say, "I will take the green plains and you go in the other direction." It was his prerogative to choose which he wanted. But so that there might be peace in his house, he yielded his prerogative. He said to Lot, "you choose." And Lot took the rich plains, which eventually led him to Sodom.

The name Lot means "veil." It demonstrates that Abraham could not see God's perfect inheritance for him until Lot was gone. As soon as Abraham yielded to Lot and let him leave, God said to Abraham, "Lift up now your eyes and I will give you your inheritance." (Genesis 13:14-17) God gave Abraham all the land he could see, from the north to the south, and the east to the west.

It is the yielding spirit that will bring your spiritual heritage. If you're going through life screaming, "I'm going to have it my way. I don't care who it hurts. I don't care what baby it cuts in half. I'm going to do it my way," you are going to live in hell on earth in your marriage, in your church, in your heart and in your mind. But the moment you have the grace to yield, and you say, "Father, not my will but yours. I'm just going to do what you want me to do," God will say, "Let me show you what I'm really going to give you." And He will lay out an inheritance for you that is full of grace and truth.

You get it by surrendering. Yield to God's miracle of grace and see the heritage God has for you.

Part 3
Grace That Heals

Grace That Heals

We have discovered in the word of God that God's grace will set you free from yourself. It will set you free from the tyranny of other people's opinions, their expectations and their demands.

We've also seen that God's grace is greater than your sin. Are you a murderer? God's grace is greater. Have you had an abortion? God's grace is greater. Have you committed adultery? God's grace is greater.

I want the revelation of God's grace to explode in your heart, and give you "joy unspeakable and full of glory," a peace that surpasses all understanding, and a confidence nothing can shake.

Let's read one of the great stories of grace in the word of God, found in II Samuel 9, beginning in verse 3:

And the king said, Is there not yet any of the house of Saul, that I may show the kindness of God unto him? And Ziba said unto the king, Jonathan hath yet a son, which is lame on his feet. And the king said unto him, Where is he? And Ziba said unto the king...he is in... Lodebar.... Then king David sent, and fetched him out of the house of Machir...from Lodebar. Now when Mephibosheth, the son of Jonathan, the son of Saul, was come unto David, he fell on his face, and did reverence. And David said, Mephibosheth. And he answered, Behold thy servant! And David said unto him, Fear not: for I will surely show thee kindness for Jonathan thy father's sake, and will restore thee all the land of Saul thy father; and thou shalt eat bread at my table continually. And he bowed himself, and said, What is thy servant, that thou shouldest look upon such a dead dog as I am? Then the king called to Ziba, Saul's servant, and said unto him, I have given unto thy master's son all that pertained to Saul and to all his house...So Mephibosheth dwelt in Jerusalem: for he did eat continually at the king's table; and was lame on both his feet.

As we study this story of God's miracle-working grace, go back with me in the theater of your mind 3,000 years. We are in Israel and King Saul and his son Jonathan have just been killed in bloody hand-to-hand combat. The news of their death has reached the capital city. It was customary in those brutal times that any remaining members of the royal family should be slaughtered, so the new king would not have someone later come with a claim to the throne.

When word reached Jerusalem that Saul and Jonathan had been killed, the nurse of Jonathan's son raced into the nursery, grabbed up the child, and ran for their lives. In her haste, the nurse dropped the child, Mephibosheth, and both of his feet were crippled from that time.

Get this point in your mind: through the fall, Mephibosheth was permanently, irrevocably crippled. He was about five years old, and we hear nothing of him in scripture for twenty years. Then one day King David is remembering the past, reminiscing about people who have blessed his life. And he asks a question that goes through the palace like a cannon shot. "Is there any of the house of Saul that I might show him mercy for Jonathan's sake? Is there anyone?"

Not "is there someone deserving?" Not "is there someone qualified?" Not "is there someone brilliant who can help me run the affairs of state?" But "is there anyone?"

Thirty-three generations later, David's great-great-grandson, our heavenly David, Jesus Christ, said, "Is there anyone whose life has been twisted by sin? Come unto me all ye that labor and are heavy laden, and I will give you rest."

If Jesus Christ could stand in this sanctuary today in a gray flannel suit, He would extend His hands and say, "Is there anyone here whose life is broken, whose dreams have been shattered by a ruthless, insensitive society? Is there anyone whose marriage is dead or dying? Is there anyone whose hope factor has reached an all-time low? Is there anyone today who has an addiction to drugs or to alcohol?"

There is a new beginning in Jesus. There is a new life. Christ *is* the answer.

Our world is in mad pursuit of the answer. Secular humanism doesn't have the answer. The New Age doesn't have the answer. Walking around staring into a crystal, humming, will give you nothing but laryngitis—it won't give you an answer. The feminist movement does not have the answer. Education does not have the answer. Education without God merely produces intellectual cavemen, and America is filled with them, "ever learning, and never able to come to the knowledge of the truth." (2 Tim. 3:7)

Without God, life makes no sense. Hear the message of God and the invitation of the King to come to His table. The only way you will ever have happiness or joy or peace is to get up from Lodebar and go and sit in the presence of the King.

"Is there anyone of the house of Saul?" Who was Saul to David? Saul lied to David. Saul cheated David. Saul hated David. Saul tried to murder David while David was playing for him on the harp. Saul chased David across the hills of Israel, like hounds pursuing a fox.

Jesus said "If you love them which love you, what reward have you? For sinners also love those that love them….Be ye therefore merciful, as your Father also is merciful." (Matthew 5:46, Luke 6:32, 36)

Grace is love that loves the unlovable. Grace is showing mercy to those who are merciless. Grace is being good to those who are totally bad. Does that describe you? Or can you only show grace to those who think like you do? Can you only show grace to those that love you? The world does not care what you know until the world knows that you care.

The church of Jesus Christ is divided into 268 denominations in America, all of them fighting over the word of God like bull dogs over a piece of bloody meat. Where is the grace of God in that? Where is the unity of the faith in that? You know, not all of us can be right, and it's a mistake to think that everything that passes through your cranial anatomy is worthy to be etched in marble. The word of God is truth, and if we can agree on the truth of God's word and the lordship of Jesus Christ, we can fellowship around the table of the Lord.

"Oh, but you just don't know what those people did to me, preacher."Really. **Let me tell you one of those *Somebody Done Me Wrong* songs out of the Old Testament.** It's the story of Joseph. His brothers sold him into slavery. He was traded in the slave market and sold to an Egyptian. Then he was falsely accused of rape, and thrown into the penitentiary, where he stayed for years. All his friends were coming over and saying, "You know, Joseph, if you were really right with God, things wouldn't be going so downhill for you."

Yet he was right in the center of God's will all the time. And in the due process of time, God elevated him to be the most powerful person other than Pharoah in all the world. He was the number two man in power when his brothers came with hungry stomachs looking for food. When they were on their knees in front of him, not recognizing him, Joseph looked at them. And if he had been like some Christians I know, he would have grabbed them by the beard and said, "Look out, I'm going to cut your throats with a dull sword and then sing *Amazing Grace,* because you've got it coming." But Joseph looked at them and said "Do not be hard on yourselves for selling me into bondage. You meant it for evil, but God meant it for good."

Joseph wasn't even spirit-filled, but he was gracious to his brothers in trying to heal their pain. He could have said "I am the offended one. You make it right with me." But Joseph was willing to go the second mile and he told his brothers, "Do not be distressed, and do not be angry with yourselves. God has taken your evil and made it good."

David said, "Is there any of the house of Saul that I may show him mercy?"

The first outward demonstration of God's grace is mercy. If you are not merciful, you are not a child of God. Satan could care less how often you sing *Amazing Grace*— so long as you sing it with a smirk on your face and a merciless heart. If Satan can kill the mercy in the heart of Christianity, then Christianity is nothing but another Bible-thumping cult.

Hear me. Christianity without mercy is like a tree without fruit. It's like a well without water. It's like a cloud without rain.

Mercy will be manifested.

A man may have money and not manifest it. A man may have the brilliance of Einstein and not manifest it. A man may have the musical ability of Beethoven and not manifest it. **But if a man has the mercy of God in his heart, it is impossible for him not to manifest it.** When the merciful man sees another man in need, the bowels of his compassion can no more be shut off than the sun can stop shining at high noon. If the love of God and the grace of God live in your life, mercy will be manifested.

Do you see the story of grace in this story of Mephibosheth? Once Mephibosheth enjoyed fellowship with his father in the palace, just as Adam and Eve enjoyed fellowship with God in the garden of Eden. Then Satan and sin entered into the garden, and man fell. We were permanently crippled in both of our feet, and the heartbreaking story of sin begins.

What is sin? The Bible says "to him that knoweth to do good, and doeth it not, to him it is sin." (James 4:17)

Sin is making your opinions of greater significance than the word of God. Some people say, "well, the word of God just doesn't think like I think." Tough. If the Bible rubs your fur the wrong way, turn the cat around. This book is right and you're wrong.

Atheists don't bother me. They really don't. Madelyn O'Hair, God bless her, has got more half-baked Christians reading the word of God than 10,000 preachers could.

I feel sorry for atheists, though, I really do. They fight the existence of God all their life, and they don't even believe in Him. When they die, they get all dressed up and don't have any place to go.

I'm not bothered by a Bourbon-drinking, cigar-smoking hell raiser either. When that man dies, he's going to hell and he knows it. And when he gets down there, he's not going to be surprised that he's there.

The person who bothers me is the man or woman who goes to the house of God and sings, *My Jesus, I love thee, I know thou art mine. For thee all the follies of sin I resign. My blessed redeemer, my saviour art thou. If ever I loved thee, my Jesus 'tis now,* and then walks out of the church and lives like hell...lives without love and lives without mercy. That bothers me.

You can "talk the talk" and not "walk the walk," and there's a big difference. You can have a form of godliness, but deny the power of godliness. You can have form without force. You can have ritual without righteousness. You can have ceremony that won't change your conduct. That's religiosity and has nothing to do with the word of God.

There is no compromise within the Bible about sin. Sin is a crimson stain, and the only thing that will remove that crimson stain is the blood of Jesus Christ. You can think positive thoughts all day long, but good thoughts do not make a good life. The only good life is a life submitted to Christ. **Only the blood of Jesus can wash away your stain and the stench of your iniquity and make you**

presentable to the Father.

God's word acknowledges that sin is fun. I've had young people sit in my office and say, "I'm having a blast." Yes, but it's a blast that doesn't last. The Bible says there is pleasure in sin for a season. (Hebrews 11:25)

Sin is fun for a while. *Sin is fun*...until you get AIDS. *Sin is fun*...until you're in a padded cell in the state hospital, trying to remember whether it's day or night, your hands shaking uncontrollably with the DTs. *Sin is fun*...until you wind up flat of your back in an abortion clinic, sacrificing the fruit of your lust on an altar of blood. *Sin is fun*...until your brains are fried with drugs and you can't recognize your mother's face and you can't even remember your name. *Sin is fun*...until the nation becomes a running sewer of criminals and rapists and child abusers and porno addicts. Unfortunately, that describes America today.

Is there any hope for America? Absolutely. Through the confession of our sins and repentance. Through turning again to the Holy One of Israel. Through a return to righteousness, a return to truth, a return to integrity, a return to holiness, "without which no man shall see the Lord." (Heb. 12:14) Through a return to the preaching and the practicing of the word of God.

The Bible is not a good book. *Gone With The Wind* is a good book. The Bible is the living, breathing word of God and its precepts are powerful. It can turn America around again.

Back to the story. King David said, "is there anyone?" As he asked the question, a paper-shuffling bureaucrat by the name of Ziba stepped out of the shadows and said, "There is one son of Jonathan's left. He's living in Lodebar and he's crippled."

You can almost hear the sarcasm in Ziba's self-righteous voice. "Mephibosheth doesn't really belong here. You don't really want him around the palace, King David, where the bright and the beautiful abide. He's really not our kind. He's not like the rest of us."

Lurking in the shadows of every church in America are the smug, arrogant, self-righteous Grace Killers who are segregating God's children. "He really doesn't fit in here. She really doesn't think like we think. They have a doctrine that's not like our doctrine. They think you have to be baptized three times in water before you're really baptized." Let me tell you something, if being in water longer makes you more righteous, there are some people I know that need to be staked out in deep water over night.

"He's not our kind. Her skin is another color." Read the Bible, mister. There is no white church, brown church, red church, yellow church or black church. There is only the blood-bought church of Jesus Christ. That's the only one. You don't hear about a rich church or a poor church. When you open this book, all you read about is the church triumphant.

Cornerstone is a people's church. If you are fortunate enough to wear a $500 suit and you sit down next to a brother wearing blue jeans, treat him like a prince in Israel, because that's who he is. He's a child of the King and we love him. If you're wealthy enough to afford a silk dress imported from Italy and you sit down next to a lady dressed in a cotton dress, treat her like a princess in Israel, because that's who she is. She's a child of the King and we love her. If that's too common for your self-righteous, arrogant, goody-two-shoes, Pharisaical mentality, hit the door...we need your seat.

Matthew said to me the other day, "Dad, why do white people refer to other people as being colored? When we're born, we're pink. If we get sick, we turn green. When we get out in the sun, we turn red. If we stay out there long enough, we get brown. We stay inside, we get white as chalk. Who's colored here?" I've said all that to say this: in this church we're saving souls, not skins. We love everybody.

"Is there anyone of the house of Saul?" David said. Ziba said, "There is one. He's crippled." David didn't say, "How crippled?" He just said, "Where is he?"

God doesn't care how crippled you are, he just wants to know "Where are you? What deep ditch have you fallen in? What nightmare are you experiencing? I'll come and get you. I'll dredge you from the deepest pit and put your foot on the solid rock. I'll give you a new song. I'll put a smile on your face. I'll take that dead, dull marriage of yours and make it sing again. I'll remove fear and fill you with 'joy unspeakable and full of glory.' Where are you?"

Ziba told David, "He's in **Lodebar.**" It means '**barren pastures.**'

Many of you live in barren pastures. You have a marriage that's dead or dying. You have no direction for your life. You have no peace, you have no joy. You've taken everything that can go down the human throat trying to find peace and joy in prescribed drugs, illegal drugs, and alcohol. Some of you are facing bankruptcy. Some of you have businesses that are upside down.

I've got good news for you. There is a Shepherd in Israel. "The Lord is my shepherd, I shall not want. He maketh me to lie down in green pastures. He leadeth me beside the still waters. He restoreth my soul." (Psalm 23:1-3) I am standing in knee-deep, rich, green grass and every need of my soul is met and supplied. I'm not eating some dead old religious experience I had 20 years ago. I am following the Chief Shepherd, my heavenly David, King Jesus, day by day, and He still has all the answers.

Back to the story. David's royal chariot thunders up to the shack where Mephibosheth has been hiding for 20 years in fear for his life. Why was he in hiding? Because if he's discovered, he would be killed like the rest of his family. But instead of being killed, he's placed in the chariot with the matching white stallions and raced back toward Jerusalem and an encounter with King David. Mephibosheth is brought in before King David and the Bible says he fell flat on his face before him, saying, "I am a servant." He bowed before David, in reverence of his king.

Let me tell you something. **I have had it up to the eyeballs with charismatics who have their own faith formula, who go around kicking God in the shins, demanding that God respond to the latest little tricky ditty-doo they've learned at the latest rally.** God is sovereign and the only time He has to answer you is when He wants to. You can't run up to God and command Him to perform according to your formula, not now and not ever. The only proper posture before the Holy One of Israel is flat on your face as a servant, not as the commander-in-chief of God Almighty.

Listen to the voice of David in verse 6. David said, "Fear not, Mephibosheth, for I will surely show you mercy for the sake of your father. I will restore you all the land that you lost...and you shall eat at my table continually."

Do you know the two words Jesus said most often when He was preaching? *Fear not.*

"Fear not death, for I am the giver of everlasting life and I have given it to you. *Fear not* disease, because I am the Lord

that healeth thee. *Fear not* the past, *fear not* the present, *fear not* the future, for I am the First and the Last, I am the Alpha and the Omega. I was here before you got here, I'll be here after you're gone. I'll make sure that everything is all right on both sides of the Jordan river.

"*Fear not* Satan. *Fear not* the roaring lion, he is a defeated foe. *Fear not* wars and *fear not* rumors of war. *Fear not* Saddam Hussein. He's not in charge of the Persian Gulf, I am. I am the Almighty God and there is none beside me."

I don't know what tomorrow holds, but I know Who holds tomorrow. Hallelujah!

Then David said, "I will restore to you all that you lost." When man fell in the garden of Eden through the sin of Adam and Eve, our feet were crippled. We were permanently stained by sin, until Jesus Christ, the second Adam, went to the cross and won for us all that we ever lost.

In the garden of Eden I lost my life, because God said, "in the day that you [sin], you shall surely die." (Genesis 2:17) But Jesus said, "Whosoever...believeth in me shall never die." (John 11:26) There are people in San Francisco giving $250,000 for medical science to freeze them, so they can come back 20 years from now when medical science has conquered the disease that's killing them. I've got a better solution. For absolutely free, Jesus Christ can give you everlasting life.

In the garden I lost my health, but by His stripes I am healed. In the garden I lost paradise. But Jesus said, "I go to prepare a place for you...that where I am, there you may be also." (John 14:2-3) In the garden I lost fellowship with the Father. But Jesus said, "Lo, I am with you always, even unto the end of the world." (Matthew 28:20) In the garden I lost my inheritance. But when Jesus Christ came, He made me a joint heir.

I want you to understand that you own the earth and all that's in it. The royal blood of heaven flows in your veins. You have been created just a little bit lower than the angels, and you are more than conquerors through Christ. Heaven is your home. You are a conqueror and a champion. When you speak the name of Jesus, speak it with authority, and every demon in hell trembles in fear. Satan retreats to the deepest part of the abyss, because you're a child of the King of Kings and you have His authority. God is your Father and nothing is impossible to those who believe and are called according to His purpose. (Romans 8:28)

So Mephibosheth went to live in the palace at Jerusalem. Can you imagine how he must have felt? He woke up one morning hiding in a shack in Lodebar, and he went to bed that night in the king's palace, a multimillionaire. He regained all he ever lost, instantly, because the king said, "I give it back to you."

That's going to happen to you and me. Right now, war lords are trying to take the earth over. But there's coming a day when my heavenly Father is going to set up His throne, and my heavenly David is going to rule from the seat of His holiness in the city of Jerusalem. The meek shall inherit the earth, because their Father is going to give it to them in one day's time. I can hardly wait.

Mephibosheth is now in the palace. He is a man of wealth. He's not wearing rags, he's wearing the absolute best that money can buy. The dinner bell rings. (I like this scene...I can see it in my mind a lot better than I can tell it.) King David comes to the table, resplendent in his royal blue robe, his golden crown on his head. Seated next to the king is Solomon, the brilliant, precocious, heir apparent to the crown of Israel. Next to him is Absalom, the jackal, who's going to betray his father. Next to him is Tamar, the beautiful daughter who will be raped by Amnon. Then muscular Joab, the leader of the joint chiefs of staff of Israel—they're all sitting at the table.

The dinner bell has rung, and from the stone halls of the palace the royal diners hear a steady clomp, clomp, clomp, clomp. It's Mephibosheth. I think David had this in mind when he said, "thou preparest a table before me in the presence of mine enemies." (Psalm 23:5) Mephibosheth limps in, and Absalom looks at him and just hates him. Have you ever been blessed of God and somebody looks at you and you just know they hate you? There's nothing like it in the world to make you feel good.

Mephibosheth sits down at the right hand of the king. "Believe I'll have some of those biscuits," he says as he slides his crippled feet under the king's table. And from the table up, Mephibosheth is just as beautiful as any one who sits there. Just as royal. Just as resplendent.**The table hides the shame of his past. It hides the brokenness of yesterday.**

Has your life been broken by the pain and the penalty of

sin? If you'll come to King Jesus and place your feet beneath the provision of His table, all of your sins will be forgiven and forgotten, never to be remembered anymore. All of your stain will be gone forever. Satan can't dredge it up. Your worst enemy can't see it. And you'll sit there, served by the best, at the right hand of God the Father, an heir and a joint heir with Jesus because of the miracle of God's grace.

Are you crippled by your past? Are you suffering in a barren pasture, a personal Lodebar of drug addiction, alcoholism, abuse? Are you lonely, feeling forsaken in a Lodebar of depression and discouragement? The King of Glory invites you to know His joy and His peace.

Is there a Saul in your life, someone who hurt you, and you have not shown them mercy and forgiveness? Have you let that hurt become a root of bitterness? It might be an ex-husband or an ex-wife or an ex-business partner who betrayed you, and you are so disturbed inside that it destroys your sleep at night. If you want to live with joy, you're going to have to get rid of that bitterness. The man you can't forgive controls you. He is your judge, your jury and your jailer.

Are you living in a financial Lodebar? Maybe you're at the point of bankruptcy. I want to tell you something, God is in charge of all the finances on the face of this earth, and God can work it out

"Come and dine, the Master calleth, come and dine." You're like Mephibosheth at the moment David's carriage arrived in front of his shack. He had to choose whether to get in that carriage and go to the king, or run for the rest of his life. He was afraid King David would kill him. He had no idea how good it would be until he got in the presence of the king.

The carriage of God is coming by your life right now. If you'll get in, I promise you, you have no idea how good it's going to be when you get in the presence of King Jesus. Your life will never be the same again.

The Miracle of Grace
is also available on audio and video cassettes.
Hear these messages exactly as Pastor Hagee preached them
for the congregation of Cornerstone Church in San Antonio, Texas.

For more information, call or write:

John Hagee Ministries
Global Evangelism Television, Inc.
P.O. Box 1400
San Antonio, Texas 78295-1400
(210) 491-5100

ISBN#1-56908-003-8